WOMEN IN SCIENCE
RACHEL CARSON

Written by
Anne Rooney

Illustrated by
Isobel Lundie

Franklin Watts®
An Imprint of Scholastic Inc.

Author:

Anne Rooney has a PhD in English from the University of Cambridge. She is the author of many books for children and adults, specializing in science and technology topics.

Artist:

Isobel Lundie graduated from Kingston University in 2015 where she studied illustration and animation. She is interested in how colorful and distinctive artwork can transform stories for children.

Editor:

Nick Pierce

Photo credits:

p.27 andyparker72 / Shutterstock.com
Shutterstock and Wikimedia Commons.

PAPER FROM
SUSTAINABLE
FORESTS

Published in Great Britain in 2020 by
The Salariya Book Company Ltd
25 Marlborough Place, Brighton BN1 1UB

Library of Congress Cataloging-in-Publication Data

Names: Rooney, Anne, author. | Lundie, Isobel, illustrator.
Title: Rachel Carson / Anne Rooney ; illustrator, Isobel Lundie.
Description: New York : Franklin Watts, an imprint of Scholastic Inc., [2020] | Series: Women in science | Includes index. | "Published in Great Britain in 2019 by Book House, an imprint of The Salariya Book Company Ltd."
Identifiers: LCCN 2019008971| ISBN 9780531235379 (library binding) | ISBN 9780531239544 (pbk.)
Subjects: LCSH: Carson, Rachel, 1907-1964--Juvenile literature. | Women biologists--United States--Biography--Juvenile literature. | Women environmentalists--United States--Biography--Juvenile literature. | Science writers--United States--Biography--Juvenile literature. | Biologists--United States--Biography--Juvenile literature. | Environmentalists--United States--Biography--Juvenile literature. | DDT (Insecticide)--Environmental aspects--Juvenile literature.
Classification: LCC QH31.C33 R66 2020 | DDC 570.92 [B] --dc23

Printed and bound in China.
Printed on paper from sustainable sources.
1 2 3 4 5 6 7 8 9 10 R 27 26 25 24 23 22 21 20

CONTENTS PAGE

4 Important Places in Rachel's Life

5 Introduction

6 Rachel's Childhood

8 Writer or Scientist

10 "Roaring Seaward"

12 Working with The Sea

14 Writing of Many Kinds

16 A Bestselling Author

18 Miracle or Menace?

20 Carson Tackles DDT

22 Reshaping Science and Politics

24 Silent Spring's Impact

26 Carson's Legacy

28 Timeline of Rachel's Life

30 Glossary

32 Index

IMPORTANT PLACES IN RACHEL'S LIFE

CANADA

UNITED STATES

Massachusetts

Pennsylvania

Springdale

Baltimore

Maryland

Chesapeake Bay

Woods Hole Marine Laboratory

Atlantic Ocean

N
W E
S

Rachel's first marine biology work was at Woods Hole Marine Laboratory in 1929 (see pages 10–11).

Rachel Carson was born in Springdale in 1907 and grew up there (see pages 6–7).

Rachel studied at Johns Hopkins University in Baltimore and lived in the city for many years (see page 9).

Rachel and her mother moved to Colesville, Maryland in 1957 to look after her niece's son, Roger (see page 17).

Rachel researched for the Fisheries Burea at Chesapeake Bay (see pages 12–13).

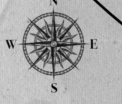

INTRODUCTION

Throughout history, there have always been women scientists. But it wasn't until the twentieth century that women like Rachel Carson began to have the opportunity to study science **disciplines** at college and earn a living as professional scientists.

Rachel Carson was both a scientist and a writer. She brought important scientific issues to a public who otherwise knew nothing of them. She worked as a **biologist**, studying sea animals in their natural setting, and writing about them. When she realized the terrible effects that chemical **pesticides** were having on the natural world, she worked to reveal them and push for change. Her book, *Silent Spring*, started the **environmental** movement in the United States.

This book tells Rachel's story: her childhood in Pennsylvania, her work as a **marine biologist** and writer, and her impact on the world as a pioneering **environmentalist**.

RACHEL'S CHILDHOOD

Rachel Carson was born on May 27, 1907. Her love of nature and writing started when she was very young. She lived on a large farm with her parents. Her sister and brother were much older so she spent her time alone outdoors.

WELCOME TO **SPRINGDALE**

RACHEL, LOOK HOW GLORIOUS IT IS.

THERE'S SO MUCH TO LEARN ABOUT...

Nature Walks

Carson went on daily walks with her mother around the sixty-four acres of their land in Springdale, Pennsylvania. Her mother encouraged her deep love of nature and curiosity about wildlife.

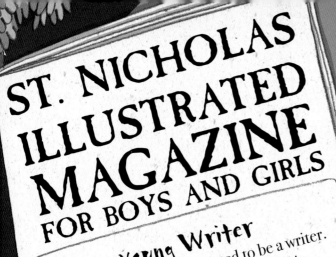

ST. NICHOLAS ILLUSTRATED MAGAZINE FOR BOYS AND GIRLS

Young Writer

Even as a child, Rachel wanted to be a writer. Her first success was a story published in a children's magazine in 1918 when she was just ten years old. It was a true story about a brave pilot in the First World War. She quickly published more, becoming increasingly enthusiastic and excited about a career as a writer.

The Glory of Nature

Carson's mother was an enthusiastic supporter and follower of the Nature Study Movement. It encouraged the study of nature, with a Christian slant—urging children to see the glory of the Creator in the natural world around them.

Finding Fossils

Rachel and her mother found **fossilized** sea shells in the rocks of their land. These were fossils of sea creatures that had died when their land was still covered in water, millions of years ago. These fossils gave Rachel a fascination with the sea and the things that live in it.

WRITER OR SCIENTIST?

After finishing school in 1925, Carson went to Pennsylvania College for Women to study English, intending to become a writer. Her parents struggled to meet the cost. While there, she became inspired by her biology teacher, Mary Scott Skinker.

Skinker's Influence

Skinker and Carson became very close, their relationship lasting until Skinker's death. Skinker was Carson's inspiration, **mentor**, supporter, and friend.

Mary Scott Skinker

LOOK, RACHEL.

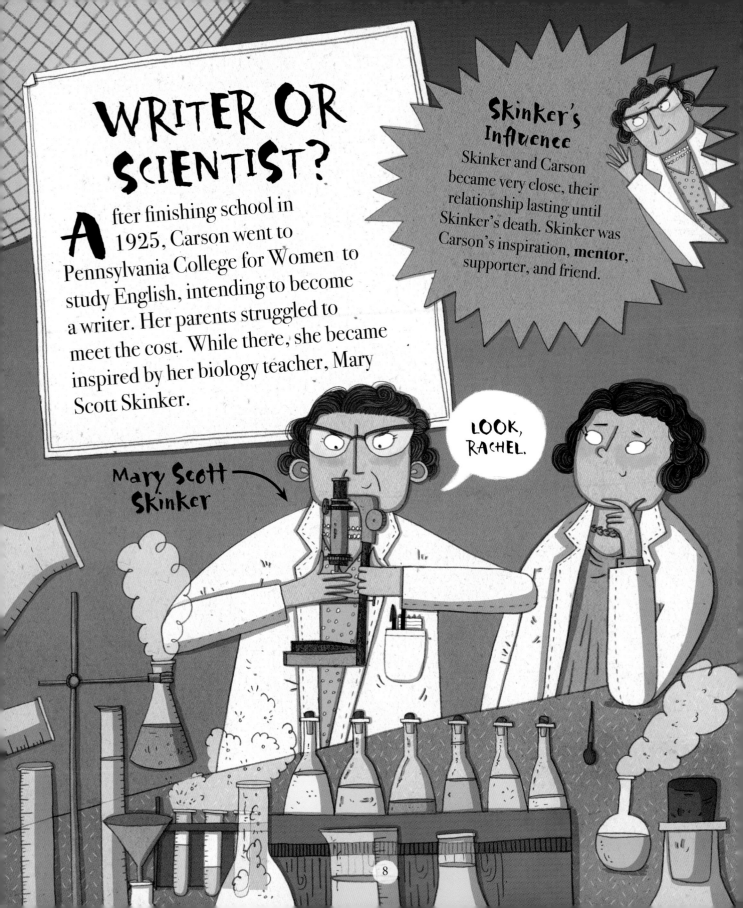

A Difficult Decision

It was not easy for women to become scientists. In many cases they had to choose between marriage and a career. Skinker chose her career. Carson never had any serious relationships with men so never had to make that choice. She devoted her life to science and writing.

A Change of Direction

Skinker's influence caused Carson to decide to switch from studying English to biology. She realized that her main interest would be the sea. She was devastated when Skinker left in Carson's final year to finish her PhD at Johns Hopkins University.

catfish

HI THERE, WE'RE GOING TO BE WORKING TOGETHER...

Peeing Catfish

The following year, Carson would win a scholarship to do her own MA in zoology on catfish at Johns Hopkins. Carson studied the development of the **urinary system** in young catfish.

PETRI DISH CO.

"ROARING SEAWARD"

Carson's passionate interest in the sea directed her choice of postgraduate studies and her career. She was delighted by field work at the coast.

Summer Job

In 1929, Carson took a summer job at Woods Hole Marine Biological Laboratory (MBL) with her friend Mary. It was her first job in marine biology; Skinker had recommended her for it. This brief job set her on her future path.

WHAT'S THAT THERE?

Mary

LET'S TAKE IT BACK TO THE LAB TO STUDY...

A Hub For Sea Research

MBL was founded in 1888 in Woods Hole, Massachusettts, as a center for **research** and teaching, focusing on marine life. Research subjects range from the study of ocean-wide **ecosystems** to the ways different sea creatures' brains work.

Turtle Nerves

At MBL, Rachel began a project comparing the nerves in the heads of sea turtles with those in other reptiles. She also went on a deep-sea collecting trip on MBL's boat, *Albatross II*.

WHAT A NERVE!

THE GREAT DEPRESSION

The world's worst-ever financial depression ran from 1929 to 1939. A **stock market** crash wiped out the money of many investors, leaving them with nothing. Millions of Americans lost their jobs, and some struggled to meet their basic needs. By 1933, one-fifth of working Americans were unemployed. Half the banks had failed, and many businesses collapsed. The impact on Carson was dramatic. She could not afford to do a doctorate, and had to leave her studies in 1934 to take a paid full-time job instead.

UNEMPLOYED WORKERS DURING THE GREAT DEPRESSION

Money Troubles

Carson's family often struggled financially and she had to work while studying. In 1935 her father died, leaving Rachel to support her mother. She would support relatives all her life.

WASHINGTON

WORKING WITH THE SEA

Carson took a part-time job at the U.S. Bureau of Fisheries in 1935. She had met people from the Bureau at Woods Hole and realized it would be a good place for her—she could work with her beloved sea and fish.

Junior Biologist

In 1936, Carson became a junior biologist at the Bureau. She was one of only two female biologists working there. At the time, men still dominated the scientific professions. It was much harder for a woman to get a position, and they often had to work harder to be accepted.

> THIS IS THE LIFE FOR ME.

Romance Under The Waters

Her first work for the Bureau was writing fifty-two short radio programs on marine life called "Romance Under the Waters." It combined writing and marine biology—perfect for her. She earned extra money writing articles about natural history for newspapers and magazines. Already in these early articles she urged people to treat the environment and animals with care and respect.

AUNT RACHEL WILL LOOK AFTER US.

OBITUARY

Marian Williams

The sister of Rachel Carson, Marian Williams, died late January 1937 at the age of forty of pneumonia. She left two daughters, Virginia (12) and Marjorie (11). Her husband Robert, who did not live with the family, was unable to take on the care of their daughters. They lived with Rachel and her mother, Maria Carson, near Baltimore.

Rachel (right) collecting samples of marine life

Writing To Support Her Family

To earn extra money, Carson wrote and sold more articles to magazines and newspapers. Then a publisher suggested she should write a book. She had never thought of this, but liked the idea.

Caring for the Girls

When Rachel´s sister Marian died in 1937, leaving two daughters, Carson now had to support them in addition to her mom. Her need for money became more urgent.

WRITING OF MANY KINDS

cooked mackerel

UNDER THE SEA WIND
RACHEL CARSON

Carson's first book came out in 1941. It portrayed the ocean through the life stories of sea birds, mackerel, and eels. Written in a clear, poetic style, it brought the wonders of the ocean to ordinary readers. The book sold poorly as the United States entered World War II a month after it was published, disrupting life for all.

Seagull

Mackerel

Eel

Mackerel

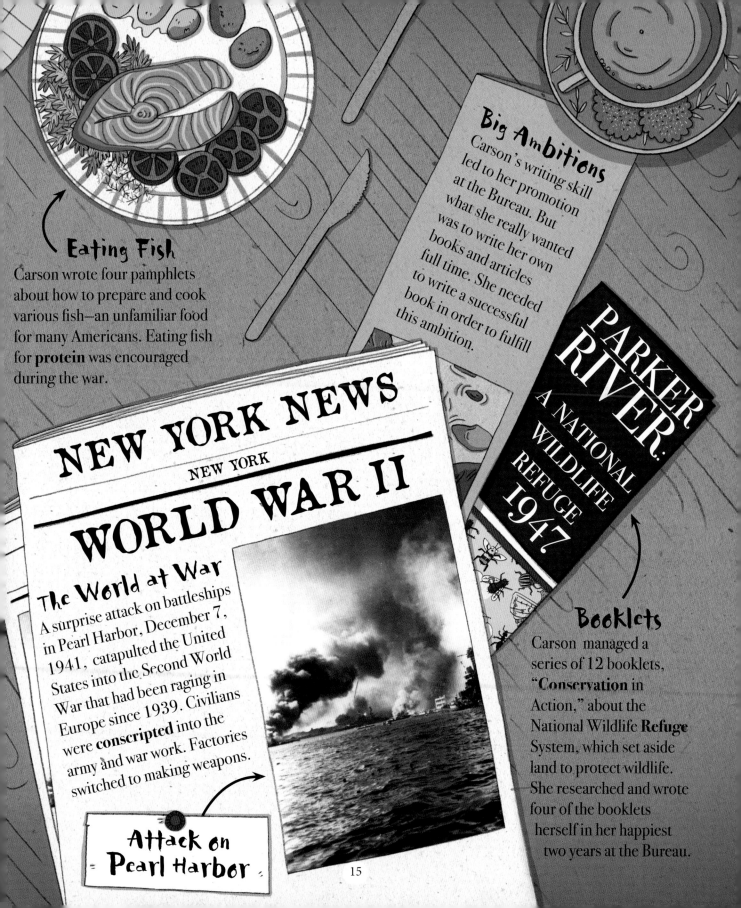

Eating Fish

Carson wrote four pamphlets about how to prepare and cook various fish—an unfamiliar food for many Americans. Eating fish for **protein** was encouraged during the war.

Big Ambitions

Carson's writing skill led to her promotion at the Bureau. But what she really wanted was to write her own books and articles full time. She needed to write a successful book in order to fulfill this ambition.

PARKER RIVER
A NATIONAL WILDLIFE REFUGE
1947

NEW YORK NEWS
NEW YORK
WORLD WAR II

The World at War

A surprise attack on battleships in Pearl Harbor, December 7, 1941, catapulted the United States into the Second World War that had been raging in Europe since 1939. Civilians were **conscripted** into the army and war work. Factories switched to making weapons.

Attack on Pearl Harbor

Booklets

Carson managed a series of 12 booklets, "**Conservation** in Action," about the National Wildlife **Refuge** System, which set aside land to protect wildlife. She researched and wrote four of the booklets herself in her happiest two years at the Bureau.

A BESTSELLING AUTHOR

All of Carson's books urged people to think about and care for nature. Carson's second book, *The Sea Around Us*, came out in 1951. The book remained on *The New York Times* bestsellers list for eighty-six weeks, setting a new record. Carson earned enough from its publication to leave the Bureau and write a third book: *The Edge of the Sea*.

THE SEA AROUND US

This book tackled all aspects of the sea: Its wildlife, the mapping of the ocean bed, the effects of tides, wind, and waves, and how the sea and land interact. Its account of Earth's **geological** history has been overtaken by modern science, but some of the material on islands and how they are **colonized** by wildlife still stands.

> THERE ARE SO MANY THINGS TO DISCOVER ABOUT THE SEA.

An island

Plants populate the island

NAME OF THE CHILD: ROGER CHRISTIE

Adopting Roger Christie

Heartbreak struck in 1957, when Marjorie, one of the nieces Carson had helped raise, died at the age of thirty-one. She left a five-year-old son, Roger Christie. Carson and her mother, now in her seventies, moved to Maryland to look after him. Rachel adopted Roger and brought him up as though he were her own child.

Sea nettle jellyfish

Mud crab

Black angelfish

THE EDGE OF THE SEA

This book was also hugely successful. It describes the diverse animal and plant life of the Atlantic seashore. Each species is explained in minutely observed detail, painting a glorious picture of a shore, teeming with life.

MIRACLE OR MENACE?

Pesticide use increased rapidly after the war. Pesticides seemed like a miracle, killing harmful bugs easily. The US government urged farmers to use two pesticides called dieldrin and heptachlor to kill fire ants. As it happens, fire ants weren't even much of a problem, there was just a lot of enthusiasm for using new methods. This attracted Carson's attention in 1957, and the potentially harmful effects of pesticide use became her next project.

HEY, I'M NOT THAT MUCH OF A NUISANCE!

War Against Bugs

American troops fighting in tropical areas in the war were exposed to dangerous diseases carried by bugs. Spraying the **insecticide** DDT saved many lives. After the war, leftover supplies and planes were also used to spray farms and woodland in the United States.

DDT BLOWS AWAY BUGS!

ANTI-BUG
DDT

Warning of Danger

As early as 1946, scientists warned that pesticides might also kill useful insects, such as bees. Reports of harm to other animals and people began to appear. But insecticides were big business, and too useful to give up without a fight. The US government and the agricultural industry encouraged the use of pesticides, and ignored the unease voiced by some scientists.

HE SAYS IT'S FROM DDT.

Harm To Humans

From 1945 onwards, environmentalists such as Dorothy Colson and her sister Mamie Ella Plyler began to collect reports of harmful effects people claimed were related to pesticide use.

Sick and Tired

Some people complained DDT caused vomiting, shaking, and seizures.

CARSON TACKLES DDT

The magazine *The New Yorker* asked Carson to write about DDT. The work became her next—and world-changing—book, *Silent Spring*, published in 1962. Her thoroughness as a scientist and skill as a writer made her book **authoritative** and persuasive. It was impossible to ignore her findings. *Silent Spring* tells the terrifying story of the unexpected journey of pesticides, including DDT, through the environment.

1. DDT Is Dropped

All over the United States, toxic chemicals were being sprayed over vast areas of land. They were only intended for crops, but spray drifts easily.

2. Into The Rivers

Pesticides fell onto houses and gardens and into ponds and rivers.

3. Bug Killer

The poisonous chemicals killed insects **indiscriminately**, both pests and helpful insects.

Farmers

Farmers wanted to use pesticides to protect their crops. Insects eating crops cost them money. They were reluctant to give up powerful chemicals like DDT.

6. No Wildlife!

As a result, whole areas were left without any birds or fish. Carson had revealed an environmental **catastrophe**.

WHERE ARE ALL THE FISH?

4. Animal Casualties

In some places where DDT had been sprayed, people reported hundreds of fish dying. Fish were poisoned in large numbers as DDT built up in waterways when it washed from the soil.

5. Poisoned Soil

The poison fell to the soil where it was eaten by worms. Robins and other birds ate the worms and insects that had been poisoned by DDT and eventually died too.

RESHAPING SCIENCE AND POLITICS

Another important contribution made by *Silent Spring* was to prompt regulation through the law of how farming treats the environment. Rachel Carson argued that harm to the environment noticed by ordinary people and scientists must be noted and investigated, and help to shape political policy.

> WE MUST FOLLOW TH SCIENTIFIC EVIDENCE.

> WE MUST CHANGE THIS!

What We Know Today

We know today that governments can get things wrong by not taking expert advice or listening to only one side of an argument. New scientific discoveries have also backed up Rachel's research and shown why DDT is so dangerous…

More Deadly Effects

When birds, mammals, and other animals eat poisoned food, DDT builds up in their bodies and breaks down into another chemical, DDE. Both collect in body fat. They do no harm while the fat is stored, but if fat is broken down, they cause poisoning. Bats died when they used stored fat to provide energy for long flights.

How DDT kills

DDT disrupts the way nerves send messages around the body. Insects poisoned with DDT can't control their bodies. They move randomly until they die.

Biomagnification

The reason that DDT was so harmful to other organisms besides the insects it was designed to kill is because of a process called biomagnification. Pesticides washed into waterways were taken up by small organisms in the water. These were eaten by fish. Fish were then eaten by predators including alligators, other fish, birds, mammals, and humans. At each step, the chemical became more concentrated in the animals' bodies—this is biomagnification.

TEN MILLION TIMES MORE CONCENTRATED

ONE MILLION TIMES MORE CONCENTRATED

ONE HUNDRED THOUSAND TIMES MORE CONCENTRATED

TEN THOUSAND TIMES MORE CONCENTRATED

A LITTLE DDT IN WATER

23

SILENT SPRING'S IMPACT

Silent Spring had a huge impact. Carson, who had been diagnosed with breast cancer in 1960, was immediately attacked by the pesticide industry, claiming her research was wrong.

> I MUST INVESTIGATE.

The President Acts

Carson fought until the bitter end. She defended her book in public and on television, while sick. President Kennedy called for an inquiry which testified to and supported her findings.

President John F. Kennedy

24

Dangerous Medicine

A woman scientist saved Americans from another dangerous chemical in 1960. Frances Kelsey refused to approve the medicine thalidomide, as she was not certain it was safe. It caused terrible birth defects in thousands of babies born elsewhere in the world.

I DON'T TRUST THIS...

Frances Kelsey →

WE NEED TO PROTECT THE WORLD FROM OUR RECKLESS DECISIONS.

Dark Side of Science

DDT was one of several scientific achievements first heralded as "wonders" but which turned sour. The **atomic bomb** and thalidomide were others. Through Carson's work, the American public realized that what we do to the environment can have unexpected and unwanted results. Progress is not always straightforward, and scientific advances must be carefully examined and tested. She showed that the environment is a complex web of plants, animals, and **microbes** working together, and its balance is easily destroyed.

CARSON'S LEGACY

Carson died on April 14, 1964. Her writing was a revelation for American readers. Before *Silent Spring*, most people saw us battling to control nature in a fight we would surely win. Carson showed we are part of a fragile balance, and that if we fight nature both sides will lose in the end.

Banning DDT

The immediate impact of Carson's work was that DDT was banned for use in farming and in homes in the United States. More pesticides were banned in the following years. The Environmental Protection Agency was set up in 1970, also as a result of her work. Although DDT can still be used to control disease, a worldwide ban on its use in farming came into place in 2004—though some countries ignore the ban and still use it.

Rachel Carson Award

The Rachel Carson award was created in Carson's honor in 2004. It is presented each spring by the Audubon Society to American women who have made an outstanding contribution to conservation and the environmental movement, globally or locally. The first Audubon Society, in Massachusetts, was founded by Harriet Hemenway and Minna B. Hall in 1898 to protect birds.

Environmental protest

A New Movement At Home...

The impact of *Silent Spring* was far wider than restricting pesticides. It sparked the environmental movement in the United States, alerting ordinary people to the issue of environmental damage and the harmful effects it could have. Environmental groups such as Greenpeace (1971) and Friends of the Earth (1969) formed to help ordinary people learn about and become involved in protecting the natural world. The environmental movement is now huge, spanning issues from climate change to plastics in the ocean.

...and Abroad

Silent Spring had less impact outside North America. Farms and fields were smaller and less troubled by large outbreaks of pests than American farms, so crop-spraying was used less. But other countries had their own problems that sparked green movements from the 1960s. The whole world now watches the environment.

TIMELINE OF RACHEL'S LIFE

1907
Rachel Carson is born in Springdale, Pennsylvania on May 27.

1929
As a summer job, Rachel works at Woods Hole Marine Laboratories.

1948
Rachel's mentor and beloved friend Mary Scott Skinker dies.

1937
Marian, Rachel's sister, dies. Rachel and her mother take on the care of Marian's two daughters.

1925
Rachel starts at Pennsylvania College for Women to study English.

1936
Rachel is appointed a Junior Biologist at the U.S. Bureau of Fisheries.

1926
Rachel is taught biology by Mary Scott Skinker.

1935
Rachel's father dies, leaving her to support her mother.

1941
Rachel publishes her first book, *Under The Sea Wind*.

1952
Rachel leaves the Bureau of Fisheries to write full time.

1962
Silent Spring is published.

1969–1971
Environmental groups like Greenpeace and Friends of the Earth form to educate people about protecting the natural world.

1955
Rachel's third book, *The Edge of the Sea*, is published.

1951
Rachel's second book, *The Sea Around Us*, comes out, and is successful.

1957
Rachel's niece, Marjorie, dies, leaving her son, Roger, in Rachel's care.

1963
Carson defends her work and defeats her critics.

1964
Rachel Carson dies of a heart attack, April 14.

1960
Rachel is diagnosed with breast cancer.

GLOSSARY

Atomic bomb
A bomb that uses the breakdown of atoms as its source of power.

Authoritative
Having authority; carrying weight because it is based in expertize.

Biologist
A scientist who studies living things, such as plants and animals.

Catastrophe
A disaster.

Colonized
Occupied by living things moving in from outside the area.

Conscripted
Forced by law to join an army as a paid soldier.

Conservation
Keeping an environment or living things safe from harm.

Discipline
An area of study.

Ecosystem
An environment and the living things that live there and interact.

Environmental
Relating to the natural world.

Environmentalist
Someone who works or campaigns to protect the environment from damage caused by human activity.

Fossilized
Turned into a fossil by a process in which the chemicals of a plant or animal body are gradually replaced by minerals, leaving a rock-like version of the body.

Geological
Relating to the physical makeup of the Earth and its processes.

Indiscriminately
Without distinguishing between individuals.

Insecticide
A chemical used to kill insects.

Marine biologist

A scientist who specializes in studying organisms that live in the sea, or the sea as an environment for living things.

Mentor

A trusted advisor who helps someone to build their career or direct their life.

Microbe

A very small living thing that can only be seen through a microscope.

Pesticide

A chemical used to kill pests of a particular kind, such as insects or weeds.

Postgraduate studies

A course of more advanced study followed after completing a first university degree.

Protein

A chemical component of all living bodies. There are many types of proteins with different functions.

Refuge

A safe space.

Research

Study, often including experiments, to discover new knowledge.

Stock market

A financial system where shares in companies are traded.

Urinary system

The system in a body that produces and gets rid of urine (pee).

INDEX

A

articles 12–13, 15
Audubon Society 27

B

biomagnification 23
birds 14, 21, 23
books 13, 15
Bureau of Fisheries 12

C

cancer 24
Carson, Maria 13
catfish 9
childhood 6–7
Christie, Roger 17
Colson, Dorothy 19

D

DDE 23
DDT 18–23, 25
death 26
doctorate 11

E

Edge of the Sea, The 16–17
Environmental Protection Agency 26

F

farming 22, 26
fire ants 18
fish 9, 12, 15, 17, 21, 23

G

government 18, 19, 22
Great Depression 11

I

insects 18-21, 23

J

Johns Hopkins University 9

M

MA 9
Maryland 17
MBL 10–11

N

National Wildlife Refuge System 15
New York Times, The 16
New Yorker, The 20

P

pamphlets 15

Pennsylvania College for Women 8
pesticide 5, 18-21, 23–24, 26–27
postgraduate studies 9–11
President Kennedy 24

R

Rachel Carson Award 27
radio programs 12
rivers 20–21

S

Sea Around Us, The 16
Silent Spring 20–27
sister 13
Skinker, Mary Scott 8–10

U

Under the Sea Wind 14

W

Williams, Marian 13
Williams, Marjorie 13
Williams, Robert 13
Williams, Virginia 13
Woods Hole Marine Biological Laboratory, see MBL
World War II 14